SIBLINGS
of the Spectrum

Written by **Denise Sullivan Near** | Illustrated by **Ashley Holden Hammond**

This book is **dedicated to:**

To my daughter, Kynzee, and to my son, Duke, you are both so very special. Your compassion, your patience, and the way that you selflessly love and guide your sister inspired this book.

To my daughter, Harper, your strength and determination leave me in awe every single day.

To my husband, Seth, who encourages and supports me in everything I do, thank you.

And to all of the siblings out there . . . the siblings of someone on the autism spectrum . . . to the siblings of anyone who has any kind of special need . . . know that you are an irreplaceable piece of the puzzle. You are true superheroes.

—Denise Sullivan Near

Brought to you by the author of the book series:

Siblings of the Spectrum
First Edition Print 2020

Book Design & Cover Art by AshleyHoldenArt.com

Hi! My name is Dex
And I'd like you to know
A little bit about me.
Ok? So here I go.

I am the youngest sibling
Of my family of five.
I have two older sisters,
It's a miracle that I'm alive.

No, I'm only joking,
I am loved and I'm loved well.
But I do have a story,
An important one to tell.

My older sister, Nessie,
Has "autism", my parents say
But all this means to me
Is that she never wants to play.

See I am only 2 years old.
A baby in a way.
But still, I live this life
Every single day.

So if you've never taken time
To think how I might feel,
Please make that time now.
Here is my ordeal.

Nessie wants to play alone
And mostly yells when I come near.
I call her name all the time
But she never seems to hear.

She acts like I'm invisible
When I come around.
And when she finally sees me,
She flat out knocks me down.

And it has always been this way,
From the beginning, from day one.
And it really breaks my heart,
Because we could have a lot of fun.

I think I'd make a real great friend
So it really makes me sad,
That it seems she doesn't like me,
The first best friend I could've had.

She screams instead of talking
And throws tantrums right away.
So I do these things too
I assume it's the right way?

And I always get in trouble
For things she never would.
And there's things she's allowed to do,
Things that I know I never could.

I go from therapy to therapy,
Where in waiting rooms I sit.
Is it any wonder
That I sometimes throw A fit?

I see my parents struggle,
My dad gets mad, my mom cries tears.
And I don't understand it all
So it causes me a lot of fears . . .

Just because I'm little
Doesn't mean that I don't see.
I see it all, I really do.
It just doesn't always make sense to me.

So I might struggle with anxiety,
I might act out more than the rest.
I'm desperate for attention too
Even though I know my parents do their best

I'm taking it all in
The best that I can do.
But again let me remind you,
Guys, I'm only two.

Hey my name is Kiki.
I'm the oldest sibling here,
So my side of the story
Sort of changes gears.

Because I do totally get it.
I understand what's going on.
And when Nessie came around
I knew I passed on that baton.

I knew a baby was coming
And life would change its pace.
But I'd be lying if I denied
That autism changed this race.

I thought I'd finally have a sibling,
Someone to play with me.
But I had no idea
How very wrong I'd be.

I never could've predicted
How independent she would be.
Even as a baby
She had no interest in me.

I'm in no way disappointed,
I wouldn't change her if I could.
I just need you to hear me,
To be understood.

I knew I'd have to share my parents' love
And, of course, their attention too.
And I know they do their very best,
I really, really do.

I know they're proud of me
But I get jealous just because
I see them get excited
About every little thing she does.

I know that each thing she conquers
Calms another one of their fears.
But I don't want them to look back
And feel they missed my years.

Dex and I are still here too
And I don't want to come off wrong,
But these years are really short
Even though the days are really long.

There are places our family cannot go
And things that our family cannot do,
Things that are just too much for Nessie,
And we want to keep her safe too!

But make a day here and there,
One for Dex and one for me.
Special time for each of us,
How awesome would that be?

Time to hear our stories
And what's going on in our life.
Bask in all the good things
But also help us with our strife.

Nessie's overcoming lots of things
And that's really hard to do.
But please, please don't forget
We're going through things too.

We need the extra patience
And sometimes we need a break.
Because just like everyone else,
There's only so much we can take.

I don't say this to upset anyone
Or make anyone feel they're not enough.
You just need to hear our side
Because we've all got our stuff.

Nessie's strength is undeniable,
She will not be beat.
There's no one more determined
That you will ever meet.

She's going to be just fine,
In fact I believe with my whole heart,
She's going to change the world . . .
This is just the start.

And when it comes to our role in this,
We don't take it lightly, we never slack.
Nessie is our sister
And we've always got her back.

We are her voice
When she doesn't have one,
Her defenders when in need.
We will always be her biggest fans,
That is guaranteed.

Dex and I have a compassion
That some may never reach.
Patience, kindness and understanding
That you just cannot teach.

We love Nessie so very much
And know that things are sometimes rough.
So please don't forget us
When things are getting tough.

We are siblings of the spectrum,
The unsung hero crew.
We are a powerful piece of this puzzle
And we are fighting this fight too.

More **Siblings of the Spectrum**

Some real life superheros!

Not all **superheros** wear capes!

About the **Author**

Denise Sullivan Near is a Children's book author who turns her first-hand experience with her own family into fun, simply written, educational picture books.

Through her first book, "Nessie and Her Tisms," she taught young children about the unique behaviors that can be seen in some of the children on the autism spectrum in hopes to encourage awareness, understanding and inclusion.

Now, in **Siblings of the Spectrum**, Denise dives into the incredibly special role that siblings play in the journey that is autism!

Denise is a mother, wife, writer, speaker, dental hygienist and autism awareness advocate. She currently lives in Williamsport, Maryland with her husband Seth, three beautiful children, Kynzee, Harper and Duke and their precious pup, Archie.

About the **Illustrator**

Ashley Holden Hammond is an illustrator and graphic designer with a passion for art. She has a Bachelor's Degree from The Art Institute of Pittsburgh.

Ashley lives in Hagerstown, Maryland with her husband Dustin, their three sons, Dusty, Johnny, and Dante and two dogs, Vinny and Fletcher.

This is her second illustrated children's book and first fully digitally illustrated book. Ashley encourages others to seek out a life filled with creativity and not be bound by limitations.